scattered clouds

D1665129

scattered clouds

new & selected poems

reuben jackson

Alan Squire Publishing
Bethesda, Maryland

Alan Squire Publishing

Scattered Clouds: New & Selected Poems is published by Alan Squire Publishing, an imprint of the Santa Fe Writers Project.

© 2019 Reuben Jackson

Printed in the United States of America.
ISBN (paper): 978-1-942892-18-2
ISBN (epub): 978-1-942892-19-9
ISBN (PDF): 978-1-942892-20-5
ISBN (mobi): 978-1-942892-21-2
Library of Congress Control Number: 2019936748

Jacket design and cover art by Randy Stanard, Dewitt Designs, www.dewittdesigns.com.
Author photo by Reuben Jackson.
Copy editing and interior design by Nita Congress.
Printing consultant: Steven Waxman.
Printed by API/Jostens.

First Edition
Ordo Vagorum

Acknowledgments

There is, or can be, as a friend once told me, a lot of life
    lived between poems.
When it has been nearly 20 years since your first (and
    only) book, suffice it to say
that the path has changed somewhat.

My friends and I have grown older, wider, (hopefully)
    wiser, thinner. Some
have transitioned. Still others have died.

I have always been terrible with money. My friends and
    family
are my life's riches. Call me George Bailey with a
    graying Afro.
A brother with a taste for Bean Pie.

There is no way I could thank every person responsible
    for the love and
support which has kept me on this planet, in spite of
    myself.
If you are not among those listed below, know that you
    will always be a part of
my sincere heart.

Special thanks to:

Abdul Ali, Amiri Baraka, Jeanne Benas, Buddy Benas,
Champ Benas, Jon West-Bey, Derrick Weston Brown,
Linda Brooks, Sarah Browning, David Budbill, Michele
Simms-Burton, Nicole Burton, Kenneth Carroll, Sara
Donnelly, Mignonette Dooley, Aunt Ernestine, Sharon

Farmer, Cody Fiala, Claudia Gary, Geoff Gevalt, Melanie Henderson, Natalie Illum, Major Jackson, Mary Alice Jackson, Pierce Jackson, Brandon Johnson, Dr. Al Jones, Jacquie Jones, Alan King, Kim Kokich, Tami Lewis, E. Ethelbert Miller, Jane Miller, Sami Miranda, the Staff of the Montpelier Bridge, Susan Mumford, Dr. Janice Murakami, Lisa Pegram, Sue Schied, Jenny Schulz, Rachel De Simone, Rose Solari, Silvana Straw, Victoria St. John, Truth Thomas, Meredith Tredeau, Melissa Tuckey.

And special, special thanks to Derrick Hsu and Gut Punch Press, who published *fingering the keys* in 1991 (way back in "the Analog Dynasty," as a dear college friend says).

Thanks to the following publications for giving some of these poems rooms of their own:

- Academy of American Poets, poets.org: "For Trayvon Martin"
- *Split This Rock*'s The Quarry: "April 1975"
- *Beltway Poetry Quarterly*: "Latisha's House of Beauty," "Frank"
- Jazz Journalists Association: "Elegy for the One Step Down"
- *Redux*: "Thirteen Ways of Looking at a Pit Bull"
- *The Ringing Ear: Black Poets Lean South*: "Key West," "1957," "Driving South"
- *Fast Talk, Full Volume: An Anthology of Contemporary African American Poetry*: "white flight, washington, dc, 1958"
- *Callaloo*: "For Frank Sinatra"
- *Seven Days*: "Amir & Khadijah: A Suite"

Contents

1: fingering the keys

2: city songs

3: sky blues

Introduction: Self-Portrait with Blue Shades On

The Washington literary landscape occupies a strange place in our imagination. Though it is the nation's capital, the fastest gentrifying city in the country, there are still traces of the Chocolate City where poet Reuben Jackson makes his home and where his poems find their roots and topsoil. The poems conjure old-time Washington. Segregated Washington. Colored Washington. The city that pulses on and off the page with the dreams and hopes of migrant African Americans who arrived from the South to make a better life for themselves; for many, coming North was a matter of life and death. This is the city that was a sanctuary for African Americans, where Emancipation was enacted nearly a year before our brothers and sisters in other cities tasted freedom. This is the home of Howard University. The site of unrest after the assassination of Dr. Martin Luther King Jr. And most pronounced today, in the aftermath of white (and black) flight. A city of ghosts, pride, escape, and return.

In *Scattered Clouds*, we are so blessed to receive this great offering from this Washingtonian, our unofficial Poet Laureate, a blues man, generous soul, loner, hipster, our dear brother. Jackson's literary production spans four decades, three of which are captured within these pages. We begin with Reuben Jackson's childhood in Washington and travels down South, coming of age in the District; we travel with him to college in New England; we vicariously experience the loneliness and isolation of being black in

scattered clouds: new & selected poems by reuben jackson

uber-white spaces, and then his return home.

Without being reductive to Reuben Jackson's grand vision of the artist as a solitary, albeit urban, black figure, there are a few conversations his poems cycle back to: music as muse and teacher ("i am back beside the/ master soloist/a protégé quietly/fingering the keys"). Reuben Jackson has apprenticed himself to Jazz, and has become an expert with his (day job) career at the Smithsonian and now University of District of Columbia where he preserves our history via music recordings. He's been a disc jockey on public radio for many years.

There's also the question of identity that he keeps returning to. Because Jackson grew up during the Civil Rights Era, you can see him working through and reconciling his own identity as a black man who at times feels as he writes in his poem "17": "too white for the/black folks/ too black for the/white folks." And then, of course, there are poems that remind us of the loneliness of being an artist. Jackson tells us morosely that "revolution is a lonely affair."

Technically, I would put Reuben Jackson on par with William Carlos Williams for his ability to pack so much emotion and tension into a single word, image, or phrase. Much like a portrait artist or a photographer, he frames moments, using few words which do a lot of heavy lifting, the sort of technique lesser poets could only dream of. Consider "sunday brunch" where the poet embraces an aspect of quotidian Washington life that seems all but erased from memory:

and where
do your parents
summer?
she asked
him.

the front porch,
he replied.

In Reuben Jackson we can trace a robust literary genealogy. You can hear the influence of Sterling Brown as Jackson takes us on a journey South with his father numerous times; Wallace Stevens as Jackson offers us "Thirteen Ways of Looking at a Pit Bull"; Lucille Clifton's lowercased, compact lyricism; and of course, Robert Hayden, the poet who embraced cosmic loneliness and gave us some of the most beautiful poems of the twentieth century.

To say that Reuben Jackson is a national treasure is insufficient. He splits open wide so much that masculinity tells us not to divulge: depression, health complications, heartbreak, awkwardness. One of our great contemporary elegists, Reuben knows how to turn the volume down on each last line, making his poems a soundtrack to our interior selves, but he's also getting us to look at his vision about his place in the world, even if his vision is in progress. He writes in the poem "self-portrait, 1988,"

i am
stubborn,
broke,
but mean well,
and am trying
hard to fuse
my passions
with the world's
conventions

The poet Terrance Hayes, MacArthur "Genius Grant" awardee, reviewed Reuben Jackson's *fingering the keys* for a 120th anniversary feature of *Poet Lore* highlighting critically overlooked books, recapping

> ...[his] poems complicated blackness before it was hip to do so. They could praise and critique in the same breath. His poems synthesized and deepened the solidarity of Black Arts poetry and the interiority of black confessional poetry.

This appraisal of Jackson's work is apt as it frames Jackson as a bridge between where we are now in this era of so many black poets sounding more and more affected on the page than they did before they went to graduate school. And yet, here Jackson is, writing poems with a real sense of black vernacular speech, which is different from African American speech, I would argue. Jackson is comfortable with all of the cultural and class registers that his poems employ and conjure as they honor all of the music of our speech and don't choose a side, instead letting them simply exist. May we always have this unabashed cultural embrace in our work.

Perhaps Reuben Jackson's most enduring legacy is his ability to stay relevant to younger poets. He could simply rest on his laurels, if he wished, and retreat into that land where stuffy elder poets go. No, not this poet. He continues to be a fixture in Washington, D.C., where his presence was felt even when he left briefly. I met Reuben at the Writer's Center in Bethesda, Maryland, where being literary and a black male can be somewhat of an anomaly. At the time, I was an apprentice poet, listening to jazz and trying to read everything.

At the time, Reuben was a legend in his own right. His workshops were always full and I could only imagine what kind of sorcery he was mesmerizing his students with behind closed doors. Then, one day we met and he invited me to take over his poetry program on WPFW Pacifica radio in Washington. I will never forget the bigness of that moment: an older black poet passing the baton to a younger black poet.

Of course, there are probably dozens of stories that mirror my own. But his generosity extends to his poems, where he shows concern for the younger generation: poems like "For Travon Martin" or "Variations on a Theme by Danez Smith" or the the last stanza of his poem "Bunny": "I'm not religious —/But I pray for black boys/ With each borrowed breath." It is in this spirit of love and concern for the generations that I'd like to pause, reflect on what I consider Jackson's literary legacy.

One of the poems from the last section of *Scattered Clouds* is "Cancer Poem No. 9." By this section, we've gotten to know and love Reuben Jackson as the musician with the wicked typewriter, the lover, the boundary breaker, but perhaps most important, the survivor. He has written elegies for so many artists and people he has lost and yet he keeps going. So we happen upon this poem that reads in its second half,

> Tonight your passport is officially stamped
> By this quiet gangster
>
> What if I die?
>
> You think between solos
> Beautiful as the evening
>
> Into which you both reluctantly
> Emerge

"Cancer Poem No. 9" does not invite the reader to feel pity for the poet. Rather, it reminds us that to be fully alive is to be aware of one's mortality. And this is precisely and emphatically what poet Reuben Jackson has done for over forty years, reminding us with each conga bell, each saxophone riff, each Lady Day reference, that our art will indeed outlast our breath. And what a comforting thought this is, because I would never want to live on a planet where the words, poems, and loving offering of Reuben Jackson do not exist.

Abdul Ali
Howard University
April 1, 2019

1:
fingering the keys

on the road

(columbia, south carolina, spring 1959)

i remember enormous teepees,
neon indians dancing and dancing around them.

i did my best to convince father
that he was tired

and that we should spend the night
at the frontier motel.

fine southern cooking
the sign said,

columbia, south carolina's best.

we could call aunt bertha,
assure her we'd arrive in augusta tomorrow,

i would spend my savings on ribbons for
maureen's hair.

it worked,

so why did he return without
room keys?

i watched the village disappear
from the backseat
of his ford.

shankman's market

"a roll of paper towels,
mr. shankman —

and a roll of necco wafers
for herschel."

he would climb that ladder
like moses ascending sinai

he joked to old ladies with
mysterious accents,

bearded men.

he was less amiable
to my brother;
clean-cut

limping from a war wound courtesy
of hitler

a man I heard shankman
refer to as evil

two weeks before he called my brother
boy.

albert james

albert james was black long before me
and the rest of the fellas; he was black
when black was worse than being poor.

i'm talkin' hair that gave the finger to drugstore
pomade,
eyes as red as georgia's famed clay hills.

it was 1960.
we were children.

still, his
presence in our homes was tantamount
to treason in our parents' eyes.

albert, forgive us.
we did not know about lumumba and miles davis;

neither knew nor loved any shade below
northern negro tan.

albert james was black
before nationalists
praised his shade

and extolled the benefits of fire,

i saw the flophouse where you
od'ed
likewise turn to ghost.

edward

he was an evil motherfucker
with a curveball that didn't.

his passes wobbled like the legs
of his junkie friends.

stardom eluded him
until he donned the garish colors of gangdom,

when he did,
our frightened loyalties and pocket change
were his.

but they were not enough.

he took to firing pistols in supermarkets.

the next time i saw him,
i was fast approaching manhood,

and taking shit from no one.

no matter.
he was mercedes bound,

selling love boat, reefer,
smack,

collecting dollars once again.

who killed him?

no one uttered names
once their smiles faded

like those bad pitches of his
we'd muscle in the direction of heaven.

edward never grinned;
not even when his team won by a million
runs.

even if he'd managed to sail a homer into the blue,
he refused to marvel at the baseball's flight.

second grade

tried to get my hair
to flop like ringo's

so i could impress
sheila watkins

whose inability
to ship kisses to england

led her to announce
that she'd settle
for a reasonable
facsimile

provided he could also play
drums

i owned a snare
and cymbal

four adjustable rings

each day I would try
forcing my locks
into action

the tight curls were
forever sleeping

i asked my barber
what he could do about this

aren't you proud of being negro
he asked

sure
i answered

but what
if sheila doesn't change her mind?

1959

those jewish boys
whose yarmulkes
gleamed like
diamonds
in sabbath
sunlight
were not allowed
to play with schwartzes.

still,
they watched our
football
games.

one day
ira checked
for elders,

darted across the asphalt

where
for the briefest of moments,

he got a closer look.

changes

I. 1969

his father is displeased
with his three-day-old
stubble, another
fence between himself
and the boy
who once lay
beside him,
wanting to know
the answers to
everything.

an atheist,
he calls to the second floor
for advice:

margie —
what will we do with him:
acid rock music,
white girls,
now this!

darn
— mother
says —
i'm out of pickles.

he takes his car to
safeway;
his son cannot go.

II. 1988

sometime between
the turkey and
apple cobbler,

he mentions
that he bought
a straight razor.

no
he continues,
i'm all right.

partially or
completely?
father asks.

1973

my mother peers
over my shoulder
in search of answers

please say
you're dedicating
that poem to a woman

you don't seem to know any

listening to ella fitzgerald
does not count

so I think of someone
call her

she says the wind's
blowing from the south-southeast
at 15 miles an hour

barometer is 30.7 inches
and rising

yeah I whisper
wear that strapless French
number

see you at 8

17

too white for the
black folks,

too black for the
white folks.

comment ça va,
brothers?

the hills are alive
with the sound of
boiling
      grits.

november poem

it's the first cold november evening.
i am out driving
and there is a hitchhiker
bearing a sign
at a quiet intersection.
i ignore the cecil taylor on the radio
to read it.
perhaps they are bound for some
exciting destination,
or a place that I have been.

as I drive closer, the words become legible.
DESTINATION, REUBEN JACKSON'S ARMS.
OH, HOW I MISS THEM SO.

i am jubilant, flustered.
squeal to a stop. it's donna!
i thought she was married and happy
in philadelphia.

we do not speak, but embrace.
i produce tears, she produces a butcher's knife
and quickly accomplishes her deed.

she is careful to wipe the blood
from the seat covers,
and wipes each finger in sanitary gauze.
i still love you, she cries.
a final kiss and that still potent smile.

she still loves me, i moan before dying.
she is still neat and considerate as ever.
my pupils lock on her lovely thumb pointing northward
across the avenue.

a lonely affair

even the most die-hard liberals
have their moments;

like the man wearing the
end apartheid button
who followed me across his bookstore;

like the woman who
interrupted me in the middle of a
poetry reading to say

she'd read tons of african-american writing,
well, alice walker,
and i had it all wrong.

she may still be there
pontificating.

i went home and watched the redskins,
pigged out on beer and nachos.

came to realize
that unlike the mass screaming
at rfk on sunday,

revolution is a lonely affair.

big chill variations

he gives me a handshake
more complicated than logarithms,

tells me my black english
has fallen on hard times,

and how he was serving molotov cocktails
to white america

while I was chasing its daughters in vermont.

a disgrace
he calls me,
a disgrace.

but still somehow
worth dinner,

a ride in his bmw,

which he swears is an acronym for
"black male warrior."

"you are the first poet
ever to dine in this club, reuben."

"that fork is for the watercress salad."

his treat —

paid with an american express card.

gold,
but with black trim.

1975

it was a long way to go
for a party.

15 minutes from canada,
moon just above my right hand.

it was winter.
she was a schoolteacher
who smelled of jasmine.

stevie wonder sang
"looking for another love"
while jeff beck spun gorgeous fills
and solos.

we danced as well as our
cumbersome boots would allow.

c.

she would
gaze
through the
darkness,

whisper toward
the man
drinking
from the
center of her
body:

what are you
doing?

there were times
when I wanted
to answer.

something
witty,

out of the ordinary,

so that maybe
she'd remember

my voice.

thinking of emmett till

stars winked
above the diner
where I asked
a blonde waitress
for sugar,

and got
threatened by
a local

with
a bloodthirsty
smile.

potentially yours

(for jeff cole)

you goddamn fool,
there was always beauty within you.

your wit and
nervous laughter,

bouquets for the rainy winters
of your friends.

you who spent so much time
cursing the mirror,

envying jim rice, sonia braga,
duke ellington's lady killing charm.

why?

I think of those solos of laughter

that heaven is hearing so soon.

52 west 8th street

(for nancy seeger)

we take sixth avenue to the village, pause
for hot dogs in washington square park,
rush past the weekend crowds on pilgrimage.

part of my tour of new york includes pausing
at a potbellied building beside the 8th street playhouse,
nancy snaps a photograph.

jimi hendrix's studio, i mumble to passing tourists who don't
remember seeing this on their list of downtown hot spots
and to nancy, who notices posters of jimi and mozart
in an upstairs window, snapping them just as it begins to rain.

by now I am tripping. i see a man cross macdougal
who looks like billy cox, jimi's last bassist. i am weaving like
a blue note laced with strychnine, the air smells of patchouli.
It is late august 1970.

jimi emerges from the studio, talking with a woman about
management and final mixes, which he'll supervise when
he returns from england.
i ask if he'll pause for a picture.
his turquoise belt is beautiful in the sun.

jaco

courtney
slugging a beer,
riding
shotgun.

two-tone stacy adams
out the
partially open
window,

grooving to
"river people,"
"punk jazz,"

the percolating ostinato
in "young and fine."

we were city boys
running wild on rockwell's
canvas,

and those were our theme
songs,

"ain't no
friday night
square dance band
come close to these
basslines,"

he screamed into air
thick with rambling
foliage.

"we call ourselves writers,
and here we are,
learning how to do it
in classrooms!"

"jaco tours the world,
makes records, headlines,

got poems in his hands."

open letter to gato

(spring 1979)

our affair is over, gato barbieri.
you have abandoned the tango
and those searing mambo themes.

herb alpert has dressed your horn
in gaudy funk arrangements.

the melodrama is gone.

who designs your album covers now? and the
liner notes about "sensuality"?
gato, you never had to say it before!

fire them all, they've buried the latin percussion
like stolen money.
were they afraid of attracting illegal aliens?

when it was humid and i felt shitty,
i'd gaze at your old eight by tens;
you were dressed in frills like a matador.

but i've thrown them all out.

a friend is coming over to play your
new record today.

i refuse to like it.

your playing on "odara" is okay i guess;
you and lani hall sound good together.

herb must have taken a leak during the mixing —
some of the old fire comes through.

emotion! profits will decrease!
radio stations won't play this album!

and you will return to me a broken artist.

i will demand an apology.
a few choruses of "para mi negra"
quicas whimpering like grieving widows.

but this will not happen.
i guess i am grateful you are still around at all.
goodbye.
perhaps another lover,
or time,
will uncover your heart.

lady's way

band plays an intro
sad as the end of summer

she sings

a saxophone answers

it's shiny and tilted
like the moon

her voice rises like sun sometimes

dips like fortune
or a mountain road

she knows
love's two faces

like i know the way to
market

and she knows
some other stuff i feel

guess that's why she's
a star

crossing the country
with a flower for her trademark

and music
for her flame

for duke ellington

music is your mistress;
demanding constant love
and international settings.

as always, you stroll beside her.

again, grumpy orchestra
springs into elegance at the drop
of your hand.

even so, there are casualties.

the years pass.
you bury rabbit and swee'pea,
run your fingers across the black keys,
dip the color into your hair.

cancerous nodes
rush toward a harrowing cadenza,
pen kisses paper,

a lover
in no particular hurry,
the music reveals itself
a negligee black note at a time.

i didn't know about you

(for johnny hodges)

that alto horn
could be
dreamy

unabashedly blue and
sassy

salty
like when you
go down
on a woman

lyrical as spring's
unpretentious
grandeur

its full bouquets
of brief
supple
flowers

the trip

(july 1972)

blue-sky
afternoon

african-robed
genius

in the
distance

performing

new lyrical
ballads

and
hip-grinding
chestnuts

whose basslines
i remembered
from
father's

saturday night
with bon ton

potato chips
dip

ballantine
scotch

and beer
parties

where
someone
was always

asking for
lucille

today
stevie sings

where were you
when i needed
you

buzzy feiten
follows every
synthesized
turn

with
lovely
guitar
licks

where are
you
            randy asks

wiping
a denim
sleeve

across my
brow

ernie's tune

sometimes
your love
is like
the dark side
of singing

handcuffs
in the form of
a smile
you offer
when surprising
me at
happy hour,

as i gossip
with a friend
whose voice is
all too rare.

time flies,
i love you more,
everything
narrows.

i am sitting
beside you
at some
testimonial dinner.
my body rumbles
with hunger

even as my stomach
is filled.

leroy

when leroy went shopping,
clothes danced off the racks
parading before him
like call girls.

the shine
on his italian loafers
glistened clear to
naples,

not to mention
southeast d.c.

with ultra-smooth
multisyllabic words
for the ladies,

and the latest romantic albums,
he'd spread his arms
like christ of the andes,

while the rest of us mortal
brothers

put our love lives on
hold.

leroy,
cool strongman —

you still
stroll through my infrequent
recollections.

days when weekends
meant 25-cent
double features,

and you were always
first in line.

r&b

grandmother's stern interpretation
of the scriptures ruled our house,

but has no impact on our next-door neighbor's penchant
for lusty tunes
by the likes of willie mae thornton
and hank ballard.

grandmother, undaunted, growled ominous warnings,
saying that the ill-fated tower of babel
was nearly as high as their backyard assemblage of
beer cans,

before god tossed mankind into chaos,

out of which grew indecipherable tongues
like those currently babbled in the name of music,

or as you young folk call it,
r&b.

battle of the bands

in this house,
lite rock
dukes it out
with charles mingus
for air space.

it is not pretty.

we rush from our respective
bunkers
to survey the damage.

a flute solo
from eric dolphy's
last tour
is drowned by the likes
of kenny rogers.

only in america,
i think to myself,

dragging those wonderful choruses
back to the basement.

in this house,
carly simon takes on
the entire ellington orchestra
and wins.

thelonius

bizarre?
mysterious?

i say no.

for he swung like branches in a march wind.

reached down
into the warm pocket of tenderness.

"little rootie tootie"
makes me dance a fat soft-shoe,

"monk's mood"
makes me sail.

but no bizarre,
no mysterioso.

he tilled song
like it was earth,

and he
a gardener
hell bent
on raising

any beauty
waiting
on the other
side.

after the dance

are you an ethnic poet?
she asked

(eyes glued to my
zipper)

what do you mean?
i countered

i mean
do you fry your
imagery in fatback
whose silhouette
is illuminated
by an inner-city
streetlamp
under which
several young
brothers
most of whom
will soon die or
go to prison
harmonize
until dusk
when they are
called in
by overweight heads
of households
who can cook like crazy
and are heavily

involved in
the baptist church?

sometimes.

wrong answer,
she said sadly,

then walked away.

changing antifreeze

i know
it is only
a simple
counterclockwise
turn of the
drain valve,

but for this moment
at least,

i am not a librarian
at the mercy of mechanics,

i am my father.

i am every calloused-fingered master
of automotive technology

who ever donned a shirt
with red-stitched lettering above the pocket;

call me joe.

when a neighbor passes,
ii nod, affect the pose of a man
for whom this rudimentary task
is but the beginning.

there is a space shuttle in
florida
just begging for my touch.

rochelle

i want to have
an affair
with your
poems,

take the haiku you read
on a late-night
plane to chicago,

sip bourbon
with that villanelle
in a penthouse
on central park
west.

or considering
your love for this city,

an apartment above
washington
harbor.

sky dimming
like a chandelier
at twilight,

slow kisses
for each word.

sunday brunch

and where
do your parents
summer?
she asked
him.

the front porch,
he replied.

donald in love

something about
that woman
changed the way
donald screamed at
passing cement trucks.

there was a sudden passion
to his one-man conversations,

he began using felt-tip markers
to write poems in the air.

wait till you see her,
he shouted,

then
last thursday
escorted her to the reference desk,

at which time i stood to
shake the hand of this
gale-force lover.

ancient fox fur,
house slippers,
red polyester miniskirt,
orange wig.

saturday night

i'm standing in a
line

behind
a brother who
picks up a bottle
of white
zinfandel and
says:

isn't it comforting to know
that despite today's high divorce rates,
ernest and julio gallo
still get along?

21st and p

the city's
in your voice

bodegas
where it's
still possible
to buy pastrami
after midnight

he pays
takes you home

turns on the tv
turns up his end
of your own
hellish rerun

i love him
you tell me

your eyes heal
behind glasses
bought in
soho

i wish you more
than expensive souvenirs

backstage

slightly tipsy,
dragging your tuxedoed escort
in my direction,

you ignored his hands
and impatience
to stand closer

and tell me
that an old lover showed up
at the cotillion,

and what a wonderful kisser he still was.

i nodded,
smiled in what i hoped were
all the right places,

as your voice was lost in the swirl
of backstage chatter.

you leaned closer.

your left breast attempted
what you referred to
as an evening-long fight
for liberation.

i wished i was simon bolívar.

jamal's lamentation

just last friday,
shirley
was my wife.

now she's
african-american,

turning her
afro-centric
nose up
at my spaghetti.

my mother,
whose feet are firmly
planted
in the colored camp,

says that woman's
always been fashion conscious
but little else.

grandmother is
negro,

i'd just gotten comfortable
with blackness

guess i'm in a mixed marriage now.

2 haiku

a bag lady stares
at a neglected mansion
crumbling in the rain

black history month:
everyone loves your people
until march arrives.

self-portrait, 1988

i am
stubborn,
broke,
but mean well,
and am trying
hard to fuse
my passions
with the world's
conventions,
but ain't no
offers for a man
capable of
singing
every solo
wayne shorter's
committed
to record
come my way

old cape cod

if you could stand above this part of
massachusetts,

you would see how the land crooks like a
beckoning finger,

how winds have gnarled the trees.

you could follow this car to its destination,
but don't;

i could see you dropping an enormous workload
from the sky.

either that,
or a postcard which said:

dear reuben,
let me tell you about the heatwave
and string of homicides you missed.

you would coat the air above wellfleet
with muzak,

when i want to listen to coltrane,
work on my kissing,

look at the stars.

my imaginary sister gets married

you've drifted into
someone else's life,
little sister,

i feel it
each time we discuss your wedding.

we still laugh and embrace after
family dinners,

but your hands drop mine
the way they did the day you
could finally cross fifth street
without me.

you take the freeway across town.

there
the man you will marry

snores, steals the covers,
but does not call you butterball

because your youth is dead now.

he awakens full of love and promises,

whispers the blueprints
in your ear.

late october blues

if houdini returns
give him my address

loan him cab fare
tell him not to be afraid

of coming into
a colored neighborhood

'cause i need him
to make all this heartache

disappear

i need him to pull some hope
out of his silk top hat

if not i'll sleight of hand

all these overdue bills
without him

transfer my daily routine

to the peace and mystery
of the grave

running, far northwest

gradations of color above bare trees:
gray, light gray
verging on blue,
dingy clouds,

dull shadows when the sun
tries to crash february's
barricades
but is turned away.

11 men breeze through calisthenics
on a nearby baseball diamond;

no one beside me
as i lumber around the track.

battle royal

this is not a beard,

it is a forest
in which my comb
snags and
pleads for mercy.

the winds do likewise
on the subway platform,

but find their way to the border
by dusk.

a month later,
i see them teasing skiers
on a "come to canada' commercial.

the tall blond smiles
before mastering the mountain,

the words recede
into the television.

here,
they grow thicker.

i struggle like
a weary boxer
to get out.

martha

they say there are no
blues singers in the suburbs.
i witness you
and those small scratches upside
the face of loneliness.
desperation disguised
as an evening with friends from
what were not always such distant
places, downtown, far
northwest.

dinner seems to have more courses than grad school.
dessert shuffles toward the veranda,
forgets something in the bathroom,
or was it the y on 12th street,
changes its mind,
and occupies the space between us,

an angel food barrier
you quietly shove aside.

june 1st

depression is to poetry

as heroin is to
be-bop:

an unromantic
deterrent.

kids,
don't try this at home.

fingering the keys

because i am fond of
plastic razors,

i cannot help
but recall
morning's below
fathers shadow,

listening to fresh stubble
go willingly,

a delicious rustle
i would associate with autumn,

before my own disguise
was ripe for harvest.

now kathleen
has no place to hide her fingers,

and reminds me of her loneliness.

but today
i am back beside the
master soloist,

a protégé quietly
fingering the keys.

in a silent way

josef's wife
takes the children
out into snowy
vienna

once they are gone
his childhood knocks

rolls in a cart
bearing
recollections

strong enough to
drive him to
music

when he returns to america
it is written

a saxophonist from
new orleans
meets josef
a bassist
and percussionist
in a studio in
new york

nine years later

i hear the result
in a friend's
house

outside cambridge
massachusetts

she wants to order
szechuan

i want the peace
that shepherd boy

heard across the
sea

2:
city
songs

1957

my father
was in chicago

a city without telephones
envelopes

post or western union
offices

i did not know that
in 1957

only the way
to tom's

where moon
pies

were the perfect
substitution

when georgia haze
obscured

the one night rider
we did not fear

someone
outside the store

with a rope-thick accent

called me boy

did he mean to get my
attention?

left those moon pies
on the counter

i was three.

white flight,
washington, dc, 1958

no more densely
freckled girls
looking dreamily
at the leaves
passing by
the window

no more
playmates
staring
quizzically
at the negroes
on my father's
album covers

sarah goldfarb
reminded me
of a girl i saw
in an old mgm movie

even though her father said that
like my crush on her
was impossible

rocco quinzani
was a dead ringer
for fabian

who and where
was i?

Early Autumn

That October, I took the express route to the back porch
Where shadows long as Baptist sermons
Shrouded the aging black and white
(With rusting rabbit ears)
And the unheated room.

My then-beloved Yankees
Were dying like the remaining vestiges of summer.
Humbled by the arm of Koufax —
Swinging without success
Like apprentice jazzmen.

How could a wistful schoolboy
See what even Roger Maris missed
From the cheap seats —
On a set with failing sight,
3000 miles away?

teddy

big ears
sad clown face

played left flanker

that section of playground
where cobwebs grew

and yard markers
ceased

this did not stop him

from awkward stabs
at perfection

size 13 keds
jostling one another

turning post patterns
into 15 yard tragedies

starring himself
it was a conspiracy
he shouted

and he was right

offense and defense
laughed so loud

we did not hear
the pistol

the rumor was
that it pierced his left temple

death by loneliness
we wondered

the morticians smoothed
all clues away

little man, september 1963

there's a cloud in your
head

you try and conceal

a cloud
just like the kid up the street

who lives on the porch
and broods like
a seven-year-old jeremiah

the occasional domestic fistfight
punctuates

the weighty sentence
he has become

one day he calls you over
and asks about the books
you always carry

he wants to know
if you know what
people are whispering

are you lonely?
he asks

as if he didn't know the answer

he knows you know the lyrics
to his song

Bunny

Tall, light-skinned brother.
Sang to the honeysuckle
And rare, moonlit grass.

He lived next to Man —
A child so sad he was named
The Walking Cloud.

Then there was Teddy —
Autumn stole his wistful smile.
A fallen brown leaf.

I'm not religious —
But I pray for black boys
With each borrowed breath.

Latisha's House of Beauty

Long before NASA
Thought Negroes
Worthy of exploring heavens
Dark as we were once —

Sarah Wilcox and
Countless other sisters —
(Legs crossed like stars in a constellation)
Spent nearly every Saturday
Beneath moaning, space helmet–sized dryers —

Trying to straighten and perfect
That which was already lovely as a planet

Distant as the men upstate.

Frank

Frank was fired from the El Diablos
For inserting Hendrix licks into their celebrated
James Brown medley.

There was silence
As he bent to unplug his wah-wah pedal —

Metal tongue banished
From their world of matching suits and
Rote precision choreography

One year later
The ghetto was teeming with posthumous interest

Frank's door was bruised from
All the knocking.

But that Friday
The El Diablos stood waiting
For his skyline of amps
To come down.

Key West

You could have
Buried Emmett Till
Beneath that maze
Of granules
At the bottom of
The Dixie cup
I was handed
(Without lemon)
Though the
Jim Crow window
Of Peach's Café
Key West Florida
May 1960

I swore I saw a blonde
Smile through the
Fancy restaurant window

But Mother said
She was picking
Stone crab
From between her teeth

And to turn my eyes
Toward heaven

Where it seemed
Even the sky and clouds
Sat

Apart

Driving South

We must have seen a hundred towns
With statues honoring the Confederate dead —
And at a telling distance,
The Old Slave Block.

(Regional metaphors strong enough
To seduce my brother's Instamatic)

Somewhere in South Carolina —
Father drove the Dodge at a speed
Slower than poured molasses,
And implored him to shoot
General Lee.

Thirteen Ways of Looking at a Pit Bull

I.

Among twenty sleeping rowhouses,
The only restless thing
Was the voice of the Pit Bull.

II.

I was of three headaches
Like a neighborhood in which there are as many
Pit Bulls.

III.

The Pit Bull paced in the dealer's yard.
It was but a small part
Of my anxiety.

IV.

A man and his dog are one.
A hustler, his stash,
And a loyal Pit Bull
Are frightening.

V.

I do not know which to prefer:
The disdain of neighbors
Or the disdain of neighbors.
The Pit Bull brooding —
Or the policeman rolling his eyes.

VI.

Rain covered the picture window
With a posse of teardrops.
The ghosts of battered Pit Bulls
Crossed it to and fro
The mood traced in the shadows
Followed me into sleep.

VII.

O longtime brothers of Brightwood —
Why do you secretly long for Chocolate Labs?
Do you not see how the Pit Bull
Sits at the feet of the players
Around you?

VIII.

I know quieter cities —
And black men with unconquered livers.
But I know, too,
That the Pit Bull is involved in
What I wish I didn't know.

IX.

When the Pit Bull strode in the shadows —
It turned the asphalt into a pungent river.

X.

The sight of a Pit Bull charging down Madison
Would make even the most ardent dog lover
Surrender the sidewalk.

XI.

He traveled the city
In a quiet subway.
Once, a fear pierced him
In that he mistook a sister's ringtone
For that of a Pit Bull.

XII.

The block is silent
The Pit Bull and his owner
Must be away.

XIII.

It was evening all afternoon
And it was going to rain.
The forlorn Pit Bull sat in his
Doghouse.

3:
sky
blues

Amir & Khadijah:
A Suite

I first met the late poet-barber-romantic-curmudgeon Amir Yasin at a party my late brother threw in his adopted hometown of Lancaster, Pennsylvania.

At the time, Amir was, in his words, an "unrepentant widower." He was sure as there were crooked politicians on the planet that no one would ever want to be involved with "Detroit's greatest barber/expert on the music of trumpeter (and Detroit native) Donald Byrd."

But then, in the spring of 2017, my friend met Khadijah Rollins, a well-respected, Detroit-based CEO and, like Amir, a big jazz fan. One coffee date led to another, and, to quote Ira Gershwin, "Love Walked In."

And so did poetry. Amir was particularly fond of writing in the 5-7-5 haiku form, in part, he once told me, because it gave him time to express himself between clients at Detroit's Hang Time Barber Shop, where he cut hair for forty years. As his relationship with Khadijah progressed, Amir's writings sometimes became what he called "pseudo journal entries." Many, like the ones excerpted here, begin "Dearest Khadijah."

Amir and Khadijah were not so secretly married in Barbados in the fall of 2017.

Sadly, Brother Yasin died in his sleep in early 2018, a few months shy of his eightieth birthday. (I'm proud of the fact that I share the same birthdate, October 1st, with my much-missed friend.)

Khadijah thought it would be nice if I would include a few of Amir's love-struck musings in this volume. I am honored that she gave me permission to do so, and to include one of her own poems.

— RJ

3 Haiku

Who'll be the first to
Save syllables and utter
The sweet obvious?

I would rather be
Conspiring to hold her hand
Before the moon dies.

When Khadijah smiles
On a mild spring afternoon
My old heart blossoms.

Dearest Khadijah

I placed my hand inside the shirt
you wore the night the moon seemed bigger
than Michael Jackson.

I told the sky I would cut its bangs for free
If it would work overtime.

What you thought was thunder
was the Universe chuckling —
and reciting a line by Carl Sandburg —

"Love is a fool star."

Dearest Khadijah

To touch your face is to
Feel my fingers pray.

August 1st

I thanked the moon
For the light on her pillow
Then whispered her name.

Dearest Khadijah

Today a client said I was mellowing.
He called me a "walking slow jam."

Claimed I reeked of aching falsettos —
Moonlit longing for....

Then he remembered the straight razor
In my hand

Untitled

She is a buoy
In the harbor
At dusk.

Dearest Khadijah

The other night
As I was driving home —
I reached my free hand
Across the passenger seat.
I imagined you holding it
Before the light changed —
Then I returned both hands
To the wheel.
I found a parking space
Two blocks from my apartment
Beneath a large maple —
(Lord, I love this city)
And turned to kiss you anyway.

Khadijah's Nocturne
by Khadijah Rollins

We share the same night —
Even when we are distant.
Consoled by the stars.

*The following lines were written by Amir, two nights
before he died in his sleep:*

What a joyous fool I became —
Slow dancing with the stars.

Cat

Stole across moonlit snow
Quietly as death
Before I could whisper —
They were talking about you
On TV last Friday.

How you lived —
Then (forever) slept with Ramses —
Your image carved in countless tombs.

What boat brought you here —
Where children of those who built them rest —

Or watch tree shadows
Spread across this neighborhood
Like a map of the Nile?

What troubles you more?
The winter wind?
Hunger?

Or those who separate
Egypt from Africa?

For Trayvon Martin

Instead of sleeping —
I walk with him from the store.
No Skittles, thank you.

We do not talk much —
Sneakers crossing the courtyard.
Humid Southern night.

We shake hands and hug —
Ancient, stoic tenderness.
I nod to the moon.

I'm so old school —
I hang until the latch clicks like
An unloaded gun.

April 1975

Should my black
Flatlander eyes
Lock on the other brother
In the General Store?

The first brother I've seen since
What seems like...

I can't count that high.

Do I pretend I don't see
Other people
Pretending not to see us?

Two brothers
Buying Triscuits

And peanut butter,
Respectively —

Is revolution
On a Sunday afternoon.

For James Dean

Indiana is no place to be colored.
(Eyes on your every swagger)

No homies to embrace
Like Sal Mineo upside
Griffith Observatory's darkness,

James Dean's rose-red lips and jacket —

Natalie Wood more distant than Mars —
And the anguished father Jim Backus played.

More distant than the pockmarked tombstone
Where my camera and I cautiously gather
Around the abbreviated screenplay
Like smokers desperate for a light.

My Mother in the Afterlife

It's 1970 again.
My mother is shaking her head
At the sight of my clothing.

She never abandoned her dream
Of a world without denim —

Now there's no escaping my critique.

(You can't have coffee with God looking like that!)

She rolls her eyes at Abbie Hoffman —
And at Bill —
Who owned the head shop
Near our house.

Death has restored her mind.
Now she's talking curfew.

My brother laughs behind a cloud.

If You Met My Mother

She would be warm
And a bit nervous

Eyes darting between
The white stranger

In love with her baby

And some semi-distant space
Between us

She who worried about my love life
(In high school and beyond)
Would find herself wrestling with race

While seeking a smile
Sturdy enough to last through

The pot roast she checks
Every other breath

Until silently
Stubbornly concluding

That this might
Be all right

For Frank Sinatra

Like God or Miles
No second name is needed.

As opposed to —

"Frank. Party of 17
May I have a last name?
For the maître d' — you understand?"

The heart needs no such pretense
When *In the Wee Small Hours* plays.

32-bar ashrams.

Peace from a boy from
Hoboken.

If he was an ass kicker —
So be it.

I think of the brilliant brown voices of my youth.

They too deserved protection —
And nights when their angels
Required rest.

I dare not purchase his music
Where my face is familiar.

For my love his sound is as personal
As stretch marks.

Or rings inside a tree trunk
Old enough to remember

All the Things You Are.

For Ben Webster

Where do his eyes go
When he plays ballads?

Higher than smoke fogging
The room —

Cymbals that rattle God's earlobes
Like kisses.

A friend swears there's a skylight
In the brim of his hat

Where notes gather before
Diving into the bell of his tenor

While Ben gazes longingly
Up the skirts of stars.

Love

After years
And years
Of trying —
Like drivers
All but pushing
Idle cars back
Onto the road —

The two of us —
Older —
Survivors of
Illness, death,
Pumpkin spice lattes,
Will bump into each other —
Shoppers
On a quiet street —
Spilling nothing more
Than canned goods —
Nothing less than a hello
Reaching across the sidewalk
Like a hand which,
Without ceremony —
Would hold yours,
As it would hold that
Slightly dented can,
Or the banister leading
To your house

Elegy for the One Step Down

Where did the jukebox go?
Its scratchy discs older than time.

Each song a séance
Bringing Count and Billie back

To the clarinet-narrow room
Where I blew shy variations into the holes
Of onion rings.

Did you hear them over the din of yawing cymbals?

Ice cubes rattling like the nerves of gamblers
Who bet on this club's immortality?

Memory is a kind of jukebox
In which you took to me
Like Ben Webster took to ballads —
And I was as dapper as the evening sky.

Cancer Poem No. 9

At a concert
With a friend whose heart
You cherish like breath

She feels your tempo drop

Takes your hand
Offers a troubled shoulder

Which makes you both laugh
Because rumors never sleep

Tonight your passport is officially stamped
By this quiet gangster

What if I die?

You think between solos
Beautiful as the evening

Into which you both reluctantly
Emerge

How to Be a Black Man

I.

I peeped the lyrical lope
Of criminally handsome men

Sunlight on their do-rags

Newport smoke walking arm in arm
With flawless cool

I was Kilimanjaro high
Whenever they spoke

II.

Late at night
When I was certain that even God was sleeping

I would try and be
Butch or
Black Jesus

Though I was sure
The style police would
Arrest me

They didn't
But I could hear
The wind laugh

III.

Hendrix on *The Dick Cavett Show*, August 1969

I'd seen comedians and singers

But never this soft
Droll brilliance

Never such shy confidence

You could smell the incense
All the way to Mars

Variations on a Theme by Danez Smith

I.

Where do black boys
With upper-case feelings go?

Some, like Bernard,
Become sailors —
Committed to 90-proof seas.

Some steal ruddy kisses
When the world ties its shoes.

II.

I have seen us plead
With gated maps.

I have seen us
Blame ourselves
For being tender.

I have done
And still do
Both.

III.

True
Not all cross-town songs are
Tragic.

But like Garvey —
My dream of
Harboring us remains.

IV.

Sweet, tiresome life.
Don't snitch on my pillowcase
Crying over ghosts.

Kind of Blue

You feel bad
And you feel bad about
Feeling bad
And you feel bad
Because your erstwhile blues
Cause some to scatter
As if you forgot to wash
Or as a sagacious sister
Said in group therapy —
"People act like you going to get all Norman Bates on
    them and shit!"

And if you are like me
You blame yourself
· The way you blamed yourself for falling in love
With things which further distanced you from your peers,
    the planet

Then a rain-soaked rosebud appears
Or your broken heart holds hands with a cello
And there is no one to see you smile

Are You Going With Me?

You ask your new friend
If she is really going

To the workshop

She too is black

And while liking her
Matters

You confess that your
Rage is high

Then ask if she will
Sit beside you

Promising not to steal metaphors
From her paper

It's the middle school mixer
With poets
You joke

Sure enough
She attends

You smile
Shyly

You want to rest your tired life
On her shoulder

Not in an untoward way

But because the headlines crush

Because motherfuckers
Hurt your feelings

Because Reuben
Because cancer
Because friends matter
In this African American life

Coming Back Home

(Washington, D.C., spring 2018)

Walk down
A formerly black street —

One which is now
Whiter than northern New England

Yet the gradation of light
Knows you

As does the breeze
Humid as longing

They hold you

Like her hands did
Once

A Skinny Trio

Dream: Iyanla Fixes Your Life

You
Need
Some
Gentle
You
Carrying
Deep
Violence
You
Dream: Iyanla Fixes Your Life

Father

Late
Life
Gentler
Voice
Late
Night
Coltrane
Ballads
Late
Father

Radio Nights

Melodic
Balm
Transistor
Liberation
Melodic
Lifeboat
Sailing
Falsettos
Melodic
Radio Nights

This African American Life

I.

I hope I live as long
As the nails
Of the sister
Sitting beside me
On this crowded
Subway.

II.

I've decided I'll propose
To the next brother who calls me
Main Man.

III.

If a middle-aged black man
Enters a subway car
And no one stares
As if my people
Were new to the planet

Hell yes
My soul makes a sound.

IV.

My late friend Joanne
Appeared in a dream.

She told me Jesus fainted
When I went back to church.